D0776892

A SPECIAL GIFT

For:

MY SWEET

From:

DADDY

Date:

JUNE 27, 2001

ALWAYS REMEMBER THIS

SUMMER · AUTUMN · WINTER · SPRING

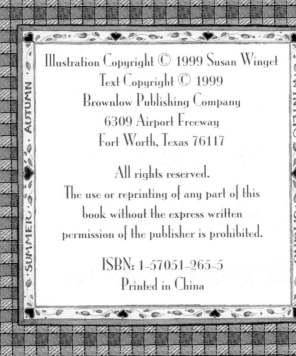

AUTUMN · WINTER · SPRING · SUMMER

COMPILED BY RHONDA S. HOGAN

Happiness is Homemade

ILLUSTRATED BY SUSAN WINGET

AUTUMN

SUMMER

WINTER

SPRING

Brownlow

LITTLE TREASURES
MINIATURE BOOKS

A Little Cup of Tea

A Little Nest of Pleasant Thoughts

All Things Great & Small

All Things Grow With Love

Baby's First Little Book

Beside Still Waters · Catch of the Day

Dear Daughter · Dear Teacher

AUTUMN · WINTER · SUMMER · SPRING

Faithful Friends · For My Secret Pal

Grandmothers Are for Loving

Happiness Is Homemade

Mom, I Love You

Mother–The Heart of the Home

My Sister, My Friend

Quiet Moments of Inspiration · Quilted Hearts

Rose Petals · Season of Friendship

Soft As the Voice of an Angel

Tea Time Friends · They Call It Golf

AUTUMN

WINTER

SUMMER

SPRING

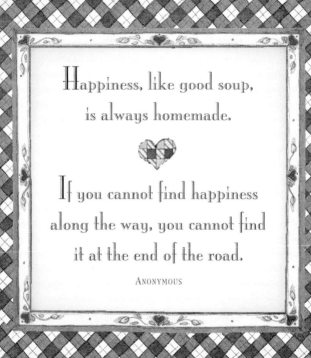

Happiness, like good soup, is always homemade.

If you cannot find happiness along the way, you cannot find it at the end of the road.

ANONYMOUS

Home is where there's one to love!
Home is where there's one
to love us!

CHARLES SWAIN

1 c. oatmeal   1 c. butter or margarine
1 c. flour   c. sliced apples
1½ c. brown sugar   salt to taste
1½ c. sugar   cinnamon to taste

3 tsp. equal 1 Tbsp. ♥ 2 cups equal 1 pint ♥ 2 pints equal 1 quart

Combine oatmeal, flour, brown sugar, sugar and
butter, blend together until crumbly. Place apples
in 13x9 inch pan. Top with oatmeal mix, sprinkle
with cinnamon. Bake 350° for 40 minutes.

A House is Made of Walls and Beams;
A Home is Built With Love and Dreams.

Laughter is God's hand
upon a troubled world.

ANONYMOUS

It is not how much we have,
but how much we enjoy,
that makes happiness.

CHARLES SPURGEON

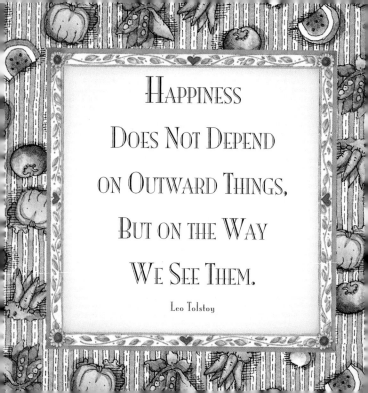

HAPPINESS
DOES NOT DEPEND
ON OUTWARD THINGS,
BUT ON THE WAY
WE SEE THEM.

Leo Tolstoy

SWEET IS THE
SMILE OF HOME;
THE MUTUAL LOOK
WHEN HEARTS ARE SURE
OF EACH OTHER.

John Keble

Where we love is home,
Home that our feet may leave,
But not our hearts.

OLIVER WENDELL HOLMES

True happiness is always
linked with deep, inner harmony.
It therefore always implies
acceptance of one's own age.

ANONYMOUS

There can be no happiness if the
things we believe in are different
from the things we do.

FREYA STARK

Happiness is inward and not
outward; and so it does not
depend on what we have,
but on what we are.

HENRY VAN DYKE

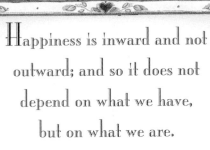

A cheerful look brings
joy to the heart.

PROVERBS 15:30

HOMEMADE SUGAR
☾ COOKIES ☆

½ cup shortening • ½ cup soft butter
1 cup sugar • 1 egg • 1 teaspoon vanilla
2½ cups flour • ½ teaspoon salt
sugar for "sprinkling"

Cream shortening and butter. Add sugar,
egg and vanilla. Mix thoroughly. Sift
flour, measure and sift with salt. Then add
to egg mixture. Mix well. Place dough

(covered) in refrigerator about 15 minutes to chill. Take a portion of dough and roll it out on a floured board to 1/4 inch thick. Use cookie cutters and cut into desired shapes. Place cookies on an ungreased cookie sheet. Sprinkle with sugar.

Bake 12-15 minutes at 325°.

Remove with spatula while warm.

The happiest people don't necessarily have the best of everything. They just make the best of everything.

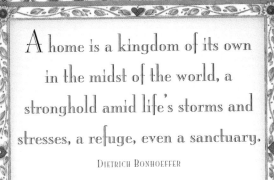

A home is a kingdom of its own
in the midst of the world, a
stronghold amid life's storms and
stresses, a refuge, even a sanctuary.

DIETRICH BONHOEFFER

THE WAY TO HAPPINESS—
KEEP YOUR HEART FREE
FROM HATE, YOUR MIND
FROM WORRY, LIVE SIMPLY,
EXPECT LITTLE, GIVE MUCH.

Joy is the Most Infallible Sign of the Presence of God.

It is in the enjoyment and
not in mere possession
that makes for happiness.

MICHEL DE MONTAIGNE

How sweet and gaily
The fleet moments glide,
When warmed by the sunshine
Of faces we love!

ANONYMOUS

He is happiest, be he king or peasant,
who finds peace in his home.

GOETHE

Happiness is not something you get, but something you do.

A kind deed is never lost, although you may not see its results.

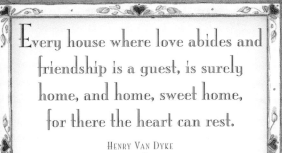

Every house where love abides and
friendship is a guest, is surely
home, and home, sweet home,
for there the heart can rest.

HENRY VAN DYKE

The wise woman builds her house.
She provides food for her family.
She sets about her work vigorously.

PROVERBS 14:1; 31:15, 17

Little acts of kindness which we render to each other in everyday life, are like flowers by the wayside to the traveler: they serve to gladden the heart and relieve the tandem of life's journey.

EUNICE BATHRICK

The woman who creates and
sustains a home and under
whose hands children grow up
to be strong and pure men
and women is a creator
second only to God.

HELEN HUNT JACKSON

6 APPLES • 3 T. LEMON JUICE • 3 T. FLOUR

MIX • ADD TO 9" PASTRY • BAKE AT 400°

½ t. CINNAMON • ¾ c. BROWN SUGAR

SLICE APPLES IN BOWL • ¼ t. NUTMEG & SALT

This house has a protective shield—dust.

Mid pleasure and palaces though we may roam, Be it ever so humble, there's no place like home.

J. H. PAYNE

OLD-FASHIONED CHERRY PIE

1 cup sugar • ¼ cup flour • ¼ teaspoon salt

1 can sour red cherries • 1 tablespoon butter

½ cup juice from canned cherries

1 teaspoon red food coloring

pastry for 9-inch lattice-top pie plate

Combine sugar, flour and 1/4 teaspoon salt. Stir in juice. Cook and stir over medium heat until thick. Cook one more minute. Add cherries, butter and red food coloring. Let stand. Make pastry. Line 9-inch pie plate with pastry. Fill with cherry mixture. Top with lattice crust. Flute edges. Bake in 450° oven for 10 minutes. Reduce heat to 350° and bake for 45 more minutes.

A small house will hold as
much happiness as a big one.

ANONYMOUS

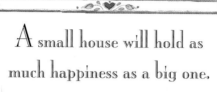

Happiness consists in finding
out the way in which God is going,
and going in that way too.

HENRY WARD BEECHER

Not what we have, but what we use;
Nor what we see, but what we choose,
These are the things that
mar or bless
The sum of human happiness.

JOSEPH FORT NEWTON

HAPPINESS,
LIKE POTATO SALAD,
WAS MADE
TO BE SHARED.

Caroline Brownlow

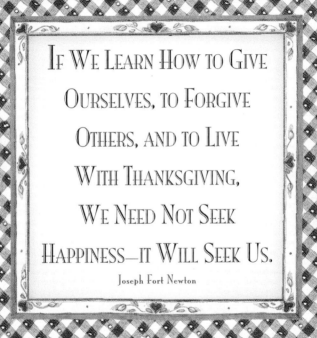

IF WE LEARN HOW TO GIVE
OURSELVES, TO FORGIVE
OTHERS, AND TO LIVE
WITH THANKSGIVING,
WE NEED NOT SEEK
HAPPINESS—IT WILL SEEK US.

Joseph Fort Newton

Anyone can have a house;
It takes love to make a home.

A home is sewn together
with threads of trust and respect,
stitched with concern and care,
held tightly in place
by strands of love.

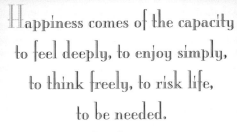

Happiness comes of the capacity
to feel deeply, to enjoy simply,
to think freely, to risk life,
to be needed.

STORM JAMESON

MAKE HAPPY THOSE
WHO ARE NEAR,
AND THOSE WHO ARE
FAR WILL COME.

Proverb

Happiness is a thing to be practiced, like the violin.

JOHN LUBBOCK

When one door of happiness closes, another opens; but often we look so long at the closed door that we do not see the one which has been opened for us.

HELEN KELLER

By wisdom a house is built,
and through understanding
it is established;
through knowledge its rooms
are filled with rare
and beautiful treasures.

PROVERBS 24:3, 4

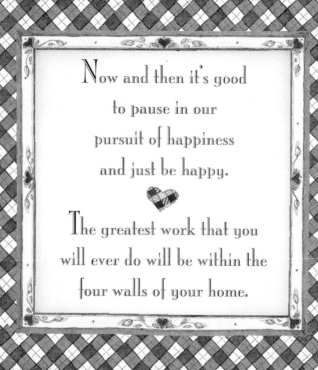

Now and then it's good
to pause in our
pursuit of happiness
and just be happy.

The greatest work that you
will ever do will be within the
four walls of your home.

No matter how often we say that money doesn't bring happiness, some people are always willing to give it another chance.

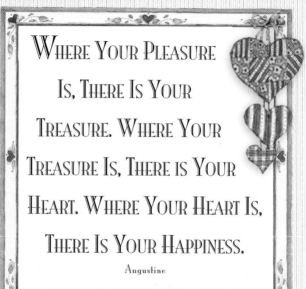

WHERE YOUR PLEASURE
IS, THERE IS YOUR
TREASURE. WHERE YOUR
TREASURE IS, THERE IS YOUR
HEART. WHERE YOUR HEART IS,
THERE IS YOUR HAPPINESS.

Augustine

HALF OF THE WORLD IS ON THE WRONG SCENT IN THE PURSUIT OF HAPPINESS. THEY THINK IT CONSISTS IN HAVING AND GETTING, AND IN BEING SERVED BY OTHERS. IT CONSISTS IN GIVING AND IN SERVING OTHERS.

Henry Drummond

Fond memories and a glowing
fire are kindred friends...
Both delight the heart
and warm the home.

ANONYMOUS

Happiness is a by product
of an effort to make
someone else happy.

GRETTA BROOKER PALMER

As the years pass, I am coming
more and more to understand
that it is the common, everyday
blessings of our common
everyday lives for which we
should be particularly grateful.

LAURA INGALLS WILDER

Come ye thankful people come.... Raise the song of Harvest Home

Happiness grows at our own firesides, and is not to be picked in strangers' gardens.

DOUGLAS JEROLD

The happiest heart that ever beat

Was in some quiet breast

That found the common

daylight sweet,

And left to Heaven the rest.

JOHN VANCE CHENEY

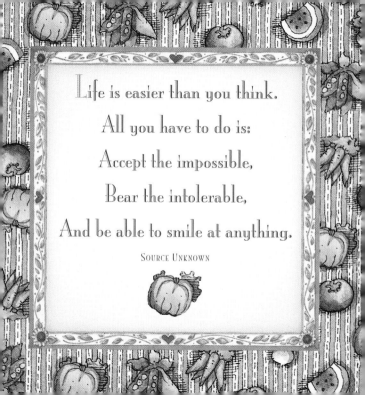

Life is easier than you think.

All you have to do is:

Accept the impossible,

Bear the intolerable,

And be able to smile at anything.

SOURCE UNKNOWN

WATERMELON RIND PRESERVES

1 pound watermelon cubes • ½ lemon, sliced
1 quart water • 2 quarts water • 2 cups sugar
2 tablespoons lime (calcium oxide)

Select melons which have thick rind. Trim off the outer green skin and pink flesh, and use only the greenish-white parts of the rind. Cut the rind into

1/2 or 1 inch cubes and weigh. Record weight for later use. Soak the cubes for 3 1/2 hours in limewater (2 quarts water and 2 tablespoons lime). Drain and place the cubes in clear water for 1 hour. Again, drain off the water and boil for 1 1/2 hours after fresh water has been added, then drain again. Make a syrup of 2 cups sugar and 1 quart water. Add rind and boil for 1 hour. As the syrup thickens, add 1/2 lemon, thinly sliced, for each previously weighed pound of fruit. When the syrup begins to thicken and the melon is clear, the preserves are ready for the jars. Pack the preserves into hot, sterilized jars, add enough syrup to cover, and seal.

There can be no happiness
equal to the joy of finding
a heart that understands.

VICTOR ROBINSOLL

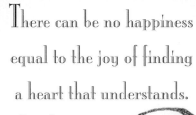